FACE 2 FACE

Encountering the Jerusalem exile living in a Babylon world

ROGER ELLSWORTH

SERIES EDITOR: SIMON J ROBINSON

DayOne

© Day One Publications 2010
First printed 2010

978-1-84625-223-5

Unless otherwise indicated, Scripture quotations are from the **New King James Version (NKJV)**®. Copyright © 1982 by Thomas Nelson, Inc. Used by permission. All rights reserved.

British Library Cataloguing in Publication Data available

Published by Day One Publications
Ryelands Road, Leominster, HR6 8NZ
Telephone 01568 613 740   FAX 01568 611 473

email—sales@dayone.co.uk
web site—www.dayone.co.uk

All rights reserved
No part of this publication may be reproduced, or stored in a retrieval system, or transmitted, in any form or by any means, mechanical, electronic, photocopying, recording or otherwise, without the prior permission of Day One Publications.

Cover design by Wayne McMaster
Printed by Orchard Press (Cheltenham) Ltd

FACE**2**FACE: DANIEL

Every Christian who has longed for heaven has lamented still living in Babylon. Roger Ellsworth not only brings us face to face with Daniel the prophet, but also points us in hope to the heavenly Jerusalem. Faithful to the text and immensely practical, this book teaches us how to live for the glory of God in a corrupt world.

C. Ben Mitchell, Ph.D., Graves Professor of Moral Philosophy, Union University, Jackson, Tennessee, USA

Daniel is one of the great heroes of the Bible. In a time of great uncertainty and difficulty, he shines forth as one who worships the only true God. In this book, Roger Ellsworth excels in drawing out the practical nature of Daniel's faith: how he dealt with real-life situations and put the living God at the very centre of everything. This is a book for everyone, for we all need to be reminded what it means to stand firm and live for the glory of God. Read it! You will be greatly blessed.

David Clark, Christian entrepreneur, a joint editor of Christian Hymns, and author of a number of articles

The following pages are dedicated to
Patrick and K.K. McGill,
good friends and champions of the faith.

Contents

- Introduction — **6**
- ❶ A tale of two cities (1:1–2) — **8**
- ❷ Danger in the dining room (1:3–16) — **15**
- ❸ Sleepless in Babylon (2:1–23) — **23**
- ❹ A statue and a stone (2:24–49) — **29**
- ❺ Firm truths from a firm stand (3:1–30) — **35**
- ❻ Jerusalem grace in a Babylon heart (4:1–37) — **42**
- ❼ What sinners cannot do (5:1–9) — **49**
- ❽ Dying to have a good time (5:10–31) — **55**
- ❾ The nub of it all (5:23) — **62**
- ❿ The power and peril of excellence (6:1–9) — **68**
- ⓫ A pattern to follow and a picture to admire (6:10–28) — **75**
- ⓬ The delights of faith (9:1–19) — **82**

Introduction

Most of the book of Daniel (chs. 1–6, 9) is narrative in fashion. These chapters tell the story of a boy from Jerusalem who spent practically all of his life in Babylon. More than that, they tell the story of Daniel drawing his values and inspiration from Jerusalem while he lived in Babylon (see 6:10). They show us how he maintained faithfulness to God in a hostile culture.

The intent of the Babylonians was to de-nationalize Daniel and his friends, to strip them of everything Jewish (including their religion), and to make them tools for the government to use in subduing and more easily governing its countrymen. Daniel and his friends understood, however, that their very presence in Babylon testified to the reality of their God and his faithfulness in keeping his promises. God had warned his people to stay away from idols and had pledged to send them away into captivity if they refused to heed his warning. They had refused, and the promised captivity had come.

Daniel and his friends came to Babylon, then, with the burning realization that God's people had better obey him. They came there with the understanding that they were going to be a distinct minority in a culture that was largely hostile to their beliefs. They came there with a pointed question constantly throbbing in their minds: how could they live in this new culture without being gobbled up by it?

All the major characters of the Bible are always important

for the people of God, but in times when the church is facing a particularly critical issue, one character can take on more importance than the others. I put Daniel in this category. Because of the times in which we live and the issues which we face, his book carries a message of tremendous importance and relevance. The fact is that many Christians are drawing their values from Babylon instead of Jerusalem. This book calls us to do the opposite.

1 A tale of two cities

Daniel 1:1–2

The first verse of the book of Daniel presents us with two cities: Babylon and Jerusalem. The two cities were separated by 500 miles, but the distance between them was far greater than that. Jerusalem represented one set of values, Babylon the polar opposite.

But why should we concern ourselves with a man who lived 2,500 years ago and with two ancient cities, one of which long ago ceased to exist? My answer is very simple: because God's people are still called to live in Babylon with Jerusalem values.

Sadly enough, many of God's people are living in Babylon with Babylonian values. Jerusalem seems to exert little influence on how they speak, where they go, how they dress or what they watch on television.

We should remind ourselves that God mightily used Daniel in Babylon because Daniel was different. We will never do any good for God until we are willing to be different.

Let's think, then, about Jerusalem, Babylon and Daniel.

JERUSALEM
We know that Jerusalem was the capital city of the nation of Israel, and, after the nation split, of the nation of Judah. But

we have never done justice to things if we think Jerusalem was just a dot on a map. The Lord himself explained the significance of Jerusalem: 'I have chosen Jerusalem, that My name may be there' (2 Chr. 6:6; see also 12:13).

Jerusalem, then, reflected mighty and glorious truths—breathtaking truths! Jerusalem meant that the sovereign God of eternity had broken into this earthly realm. He had taken up residence there. We can go further. Jerusalem meant that the God of grace had found people in their sins, forgiven them and appointed them to live according to his laws and for his glory.

Jerusalem was the place of the temple, and the temple was the place of sacrifices, all of which were designed to point to the supreme sacrifice that the Lord Jesus Christ would offer on the cross.

Jerusalem represented, then, the glorious God graciously purchasing guilty sinners through the shedding of the blood of his Son and instilling in them a passion to live for his glory. And Jerusalem represents something else: those whom God graciously visits and saves today will enter the heavenly Jerusalem when this life is over.

Do you have Jerusalem in your life? Every Christian does. The author of Hebrews states, 'But you have come to Mount Zion and to the city of the living God, the heavenly Jerusalem' (Heb. 12:22). I can tell you this: if Jerusalem is in your life, it will be the main thing in your life; if it is not the main thing, it is not in your life.

Jerusalem had such a hold on Daniel; he could not get over it! He would gladly have taken as his own these words of the psalmist:

> If I forget you, O Jerusalem,
> Let my right hand forget its skill!
> If I do not remember you,
> Let my tongue cling to the roof of my mouth—
> If I do not exalt Jerusalem
> Above my chief joy. (Ps. 137:5–6)

The crying need of the hour is for Jerusalem to grip us as it did Daniel.

BABYLON

When Daniel was still very young, the most traumatic thing imaginable happened. The Babylonian army invaded the land of Judah and carried many of its citizens away captive. This occurred in 605 BC. The Babylonians would return in 586 BC and completely destroy the city of Jerusalem and its glorious temple. So, at a tender age, Daniel was violently ripped away from everything that he knew and loved.

In Babylon he and three of his friends were stationed at the king's palace for one purpose. King Nebuchadnezzar was going to make good Babylonians out of them. Geoff Thomas says that Nebuchadnezzar was out to make sure that Daniel and his friends were 'utterly marinated in Babylonian ideals, assimilating that culture's whole way of life and values, forgetting all their past. What they laughed about, and what they would lay down their lives for, would henceforth be Babylonian.'[1]

We have to hand it to the Babylonians. They were very shrewd. Thomas states their strategy in these words: 'we'll get them when they are young, and then in their whole lives they will serve us.'²

The Babylonians haven't changed with the passing of the years. They are still after our children, and they are having remarkable success!

What was wrong with Daniel going along with the programme? Daniel saw the issue clearly. Babylon represented many things that were opposed to Jerusalem, and to embrace those things would be to repudiate Jerusalem.

Babylon testified to many gods; Jerusalem to the one and only God, the Maker of heaven and earth and Ruler of the same. Babylon testified to man and what he could accomplish through his own power and wisdom. Jerusalem gave testimony to the helplessness of man and his radical need for the grace of God. Babylon testified to the here and now; Jerusalem to eternity. Babylon testified to living for the purpose of gratifying the flesh; Jerusalem to living for the glory of God.

It was not a matter of Babylon being wrong on every single issue; Daniel was happy to embrace various parts of that culture. It was rather a matter of Babylon often claiming the same territory as Jerusalem. At those points, Daniel chose Jerusalem. While Daniel lived *in* Babylon, he would live *for* Jerusalem!

Babylon and Jerusalem: they are still with us! We are all living in the former. Are we living for the latter?

A DILEMMA

You may think that I have painted myself in a corner. I have been talking about what Babylon represented and what

Jerusalem represented, and affirming that the latter is far superior to the former. And you may find yourself wanting to say, 'Don't you realize that Babylon conquered Jerusalem? If Jerusalem represents God and good, and Babylon represents evil, then we must say that evil will conquer God and good.'

It often seems so! It may very well have seemed that way to Daniel. As he looked at the power and the beauty of Babylon, it may have appeared to him that she was invincible.

But outward appearances are often deceiving, and Babylon, with all her might and all her wisdom, would not last. She had her brief appearance on the stage of human history as the world's greatest power, and then she fell to the Persians. And Daniel's people returned to their homeland and Jerusalem rose from the ashes. Babylon went from glory to ashes, and Jerusalem went from ashes to glory.

By the way, the fact that Babylon conquered Jerusalem does not mean that God was defeated or discredited. The defeat of Jerusalem and the victory of Babylon proved the sovereignty of God and his faithfulness to his promises. The Babylonians succeeded only because God used them as his instrument of judgement on the sins of his people.

In our own modern Babylon, it seems to be utter folly for any pastor to call his people to live for Jerusalem. Ours is a world that makes it appear as if there is no hope at all for the cause of Christ.

What are we to do in this world? Go ahead and live for Christ! The book of Revelation enables us to peer down the corridor of time and see what awaits Babylon: 'her plagues will come in one day—death and mourning and famine. And she will be utterly burned with fire, for strong is the Lord God who judges her' (Rev. 18:8). The Babylon that hates God will eventually be judged by God, and on that day those who loved her will cry, 'Alas, alas, that great city Babylon, that mighty city! For in one hour your judgment has come' (Rev. 18:10). And this book of Revelation closes by telling us that the 'New Jerusalem' will come down 'out of heaven from God' (Rev. 21:2).

The upshot of it all is this: those who live for Babylon are going to lose it all, and those who live for Jerusalem are going to gain eternal glory. So let us join Daniel in living for Jerusalem. Let us not be deceived by Babylon and all her enticements and seductive allurements. Babylon is going to fail, and Jerusalem is going to last!

FOR FURTHER STUDY

1. Read 1 John 2:15–17. What do these verses teach us about loving the world? What will ultimately happen to this world?
2. Read 2 Corinthians 6:14–7:1. What does Paul say about Christians and their relationship with the world? What does it mean to 'be separate' (v. 17)?

TO THINK ABOUT AND DISCUSS

1. What is our society doing to 'Babylonianize' Christians? What are the particular temptations that face Christians of different age groups: younger Christians? older Christians?
2. What can you do to minimize the effects of Babylon and maximize the influence of Jerusalem on your life? How can you train yourself to recognize the effects of Babylon in the first place?

Notes

1 **Geoff Thomas,** *Daniel: Servant of God under Four Kings* (Bridgend: Bryntirion, 1998), p. 15.
2 Ibid. p. 14.

2 Danger in the dining room

Daniel 1:3–16

When Daniel was a young man, the army of Nebuchadnezzar came into Jerusalem, took him and many others captive and carried them back to Babylon. There Daniel was placed in the king's court. If Nebuchadnezzar could make Babylonians out of Daniel and his friends, they would be useful to him in controlling the other captives from Jerusalem.

But Nebuchadnezzar soon found that these young men would not be easily 'Babylonianized'. Even though they were in Babylon, their hearts were in Jerusalem. More importantly, Jerusalem was in them.

We are studying the life of Daniel because we find ourselves in much the same position as he. Christians today live in Babylon. We live in a world that is opposed to God and is intoxicated with man. We live in a world that worships many gods, dismisses thoughts of eternity and emphasizes gratifying the flesh.

But while we are in this world, we are called to live with Jerusalem values. We are called to live for the God who has invaded our hearts and made us his own. We are called to live in such a way that we give evidence of having been thrilled by God.

Sadly enough, many Christians are failing. They are living

as Babylonians in this Babylonian world. Because all of us are so inclined in this direction, we must ever keep the example of Daniel before our eyes.

Daniel 1:3–16 shows how Daniel and his friends demonstrated Jerusalem values on the issue of food. They were enrolled in a special school that would train them to serve the king (v. 5), and Babylonian food was placed before them. It all sounds so innocent and harmless. Daniel and his friends were in Babylon; why not eat Babylonian food? But Daniel saw danger in that dining room! Let's consider both the nature of that danger and Daniel's response to it.

WHY THE FOOD WAS DANGEROUS

It is interesting that Daniel and his friends were given Babylonian names, and they did not object. Why? God's people cannot control what they are called! Flaming fundies! Goody Two-Shoes! Holy Joes! The God-squad! God's people have been called all of these and more. But what can we do?

On the matter of food, however, Daniel and his friends could do something. They could refuse to eat!

Why did they make an issue of this? What did they find objectionable about the food? The answer is that the food had been offered to idols before it was served. Stuart Olyott explains, 'Every Babylonian kingly meal began with an act of pagan worship. They were a lot more diligent about this than many Christians are about saying grace before eating. Nothing was eaten and nothing was drunk until it was dedicated to certain pagan deities. Those who ate the food were reckoned to have participated in pagan rites.'[1]

Why were Daniel and his friends so scrupulous about food

offered to idols? They knew that they were in Babylon because of idolatry! Stuart Olyott says of the Jewish people, 'The crying sin had been idolatry. The exile was a punishment for all of the nation's sins, but for that one in particular, and they were to remain in Babylon until they had finished with it for ever.'[2]

We make a grave error if we think that idolatry is a thing of the past. If we think it is merely a matter of painting a funny face on a rock or piece of wood and bowing down before it, we are dead wrong! Idolatry is giving to anything the devotion and allegiance that belong to God. It is diverting anything that properly belongs to God to something or someone else.

Do we take idolatry seriously? We will do so only to the extent that we realize how very much God has done for us. Through his Son, Jesus Christ, he has forgiven us our sins, delivered us from wrath to come and given us the title to eternal glory. How can we not love this God? How can we be so ungrateful as to give to other things the love and devotion that belong to him?

HOW DANIEL RESPONDED

The pressure on Daniel was intense. Political pressure, the chance to move ahead of the other young men, was there. Peer pressure, the pressure to do what everyone was doing, was there. Religious pressure was also there. The fact that Daniel and his friends were in captivity seemed to indicate that their God had failed and the gods of the Babylonians had prevailed. Why not, in light of this, renounce their God and go along with the worship of the Babylonian gods?

Yet, although the pressure was enormous, Daniel refused to

yield. How did he manage to resist such enormous pressure? The answer is given in these words: 'Daniel purposed in his heart that he would not defile himself ...' (v. 8). He saw that the real battlefield was in his heart, not in Babylon, and he won the battle there before he won it in Babylon.

Does this mean that Daniel was simply one of those rare men who are able, through iron will and steadfast determination, to carry out what they resolve to do? There can be no doubt that determination to carry out resolve was present, but there is more than that here. Daniel's resolve was fed by something else. It was the realization that he was not, in the final analysis, a citizen of the kingdom of Babylon or the kingdom of Judah, but rather of a far greater kingdom—the kingdom of heaven. And his sovereign was not Nebuchadnezzar or any other earthly ruler, but rather 'the God of heaven' (2:18–19, 28, 37, 44).

Daniel spoke to his friends of this God in this way:

... wisdom and might are His.
And He changes the times and the seasons;
He removes kings and raises up kings;
He gives wisdom to the wise
And knowledge to those who have understanding.
He reveals deep and secret things;
He knows what is in the darkness,
And light dwells with Him.   (Dan. 2:20b–22)

Realizing there is such a God in heaven changes everything here on earth. Such a God can be trusted to protect and vindicate his people when they take a stand for him.

Trust is exactly what Daniel and his friends did. They requested that they be given ten days to go without the king's food and then be judged as to whether they were worse off than those who did eat the king's food (vv. 11–13). After those days, Daniel and his friends were interviewed by the king himself. And the king's testimony was that there was 'none equal' to them (v. 19, NIV).

Daniel let it be known that he and his friends were taking their stand against Babylonian food because of their God. The fact that they surpassed all the other young men in Babylon brought glory to God.

Daniel stands before us as a shining example of what we should be doing. We should be living for God in such a way that even unbelievers will have to say of us, 'These Christians have no equal.'

A Christian should be the best employee an employer has. Christian young people should be the best students in the school. Christians should be the best patients in the hospital. Christians should be the best members of their families. There should be no one like us in language, in kindness, in moral virtue, in dependability and trustworthiness, in dress.

Babylon is not going to be changed by signing petitions or by lecturing Babylonians for being Babylonians. It can only be changed by Christians being Christians.

In all these things Daniel serves as a picture of the Lord Jesus Christ. He came to this Babylonian world, refused to be defiled by it, and lived in perfect obedience to God. Then he went to the cross to receive the penalty for sinners so all who believe will not have to receive that penalty themselves. Now the glad testimony of all those who know Jesus is this: there is none equal to him.

FACE2FACE: DANIEL

WHAT IT HAS TO DO WITH US

It should be obvious that Christians today are in a situation very similar to the one in which Daniel and his friends found themselves. We're also a minority group within a culture that is often hostile to the things of God.

The question before us is the same as the one confronting those men, namely, how do we live in this culture without being eaten up by it?

Many professing Christians seem to have answered the question by caving in at every point. They uncritically accept all that our own modern-day Babylon has to offer. They think like the Babylonians, talk like them and act like them. Everything about them is more Babylonian than it is Christian.

But merely calling oneself a Christian doesn't make one so, and those who have comfortably settled in with the Babylonians only show their true colours. It is impossible for Christians to be completely at ease in a world such as this. For them the age-old question remains: how does one live as a Christian in a Babylonian world?

The ability to stay true to God in our own Babylon comes only as we purpose in our hearts to be true, and we can only do that if we take a long and ruthless look at the competing kingdoms.

Take a look at Babylon. Yes, there is much about it that is attractive and appealing—things which God's people are free to enjoy when they do not conflict with God's Word—but with all its attractiveness and appeal, the kingdom of Babylon is a kingdom only of this world and will finally pass away.

Now take a look at God's kingdom. That kingdom offers beauties and glories that make the beauties of this world seem dull and dim, and that kingdom endures for ever. Nebuchadnezzar himself would eventually acknowledge this truth, saying of the Lord, 'His dominion is an everlasting dominion, and His kingdom is from generation to generation' (4:34).

We will never be able to stand in our own Babylon until we realize that we are citizens of a far greater kingdom, one that will never pass away. And the God of that kingdom can be trusted to strengthen and help us even in the face of enormous pressure.

How do we know there is such a kingdom? Is it just a figment of our imagination, a mere will-o'-the-wisp, a product of wishful thinking? Thank God, it is far more certain than that. We know there is such a kingdom because one came from there, lived among us, died for us, arose from the grave and returned to heaven—the Lord Jesus Christ. When we stop to ponder who he is and what he has done for us, we not only realize the reality of the kingdom of heaven, but we most certainly also find ourselves desiring to live in this Babylon in a way that brings glory to him.

FOR FURTHER STUDY

1. Read Philippians 3:20–21. What does Paul say in these verses about the Christian's citizenship?
2. Read Hebrews 11:8–16. How are Christians to live in this world? What is the hope that spurs us on to live this way?

TO THINK ABOUT AND DISCUSS

1. Do you agree that many Christians appear to be more influenced by Babylon than by Jerusalem? If so, what is the evidence for this? Why are so many Christians enticed by this world when they have such a wonderful kingdom to look forward to?
2. Identify some issues where the world demands Christians' compliance but such compliance would be idolatry. Think of situations Christians may face in the workplace and among friends and family, as well as issues connected with 'political correctness'. Have you experienced a situation like this? If so, how did you handle it?

Notes

1 **Stuart Olyott,** *Dare to Stand Alone* (Welwyn: Evangelical Press, 1982), p. 20.
2 Ibid. p. 16.

3 Sleepless in Babylon

Daniel 2:1–23

King Nebuchadnezzar of Babylon had a serious problem on his hands. He kept dreaming the same dream, and it was such a troubling dream that he couldn't sleep (v. 1).

He had magicians, astrologers and sorcerers to help him with such matters, so he called them in. But he had come to know the manner in which these men operated. He would tell them his dream, and they would craft an interpretation. And the interpretation would be such that they would be able to claim that it had come true no matter what happened.

Having had enough of this business and earnestly desiring the true interpretation of his dream, Nebuchadnezzar decided to do things differently. He would not tell his 'wise men' what he had dreamed. They would tell him! And they would then give the interpretation (vv. 8–9). When these men protested, Nebuchadnezzar began putting them to death (vv. 10–13).

By this time, Daniel and his friends had risen to the level of being 'wise men' in Nebuchadnezzar's court. So the decree of death included them (v. 13). When Daniel learned of these developments, he appealed to the king to give him time to discern the dream and its interpretation (v. 16). Daniel then gathered his friends to pray, and God graciously gave him both the dream and the interpretation.

A king having a dream! A king executing people! The dream being interpreted! What does it all have to do with us? No one had a cellphone or an iPod. There was no MySpace. Surely this old story has no value for us?

But perhaps we need to think again. This ancient episode actually contains principles that are just as vital today as they were in old Babylon. The first principle is this:

GOD IS AT WORK IN THIS WORLD

It did not appear to be so. The only people who believed in the God of the Bible were the Jews, and many of them were in Babylon, which was the place of many gods. It looked as if God had been thoroughly discredited. What kind of God is it that cannot protect the city devoted to his honour and keep his people out of captivity?

Babylon, on the other hand, was an exciting place. It was powerful, successful and prosperous. The gods of Babylon seemed to have achieved for their adherents everything that the God of Israel had failed to achieve for his.

But the Bible constantly tells us that things are not always as they appear, and the world has often showed up for God's funeral only to find that the corpse was not present!

So here is Nebuchadnezzar in the midst of his Babylon, secure in his belief that his ideas and his ways are correct and the God of little defeated Judah is nothing at all. But here also is this dream, and it is deeply troubling—so much so that the man can't sleep. If it were the dream of one night, it could easily have been dismissed. But it is the dream of every night, and Nebuchadnezzar earnestly desires to sleep because he is so tired, but he is afraid to sleep because of the dream that preys on him.

How are we to explain this recurring and terrifying dream? This account leaves no doubt. It is from the 'discredited' God of little Judah (vv. 18–23, 28–30)! Perhaps this God is not powerless after all! He can plant a dream in a king's head, and it won't go away.

Now keep this thought with you: God is always at work in his world! And often his work consists of doing something very little which will finally prove to be very big!

A second lesson that emerges from this account is this:

LEFT TO THEMSELVES, MEN AND WOMEN ARE COMPLETELY HELPLESS IN REGARD TO THE THINGS OF GOD

Nebuchadnezzar did not realize it at the beginning, but he had a message from the true God on his hands. God was speaking to him in that dream! And he was speaking a message of monumental significance.

But Nebuchadnezzar couldn't figure it out. He had no idea what it was all about. He was both sleepless and clueless! He called in his helpers, and they were equally helpless!

So how did Nebuchadnezzar come to understand the dream? He did so through the mediator that God provided for him—Daniel! Ronald S. Wallace writes, 'The main point in the story is that Daniel at this moment becomes a key man. He alone is able to act decisively and shrewdly where others are hopelessly incapable and benumbed. By an act of solitary leadership he is able to prevent the disaster threatening both Nebuchadnezzar and his counsellors.'[1]

The helplessness of Nebuchadnezzar and his advisors represents the helplessness of us all in spiritual things. How helpless are we? Totally! The Bible tells us that our minds are so darkened that we cannot understand the truth of God (1 Cor. 2:14) and our wills are so deadened that we cannot come to God (Eph. 2:1–3).

But the fact that we are helpless does not mean we are hopeless. As God sent Daniel to help Nebuchadnezzar, so he has sent his Son to provide salvation for sinners and the Holy Spirit to apply that salvation to sinners.

All of this is due to grace. The God who did not have to do anything for us has done everything for us. That brings us to a third and final lesson:

DANIEL'S EXPERIENCE WITH NEBUCHADNEZZAR TEACHES US WHERE TO TURN IN A TROUBLED, THREATENING WORLD

There can be no doubt that Daniel and his friends were living in a very threatening world. Nebuchadnezzar was intending to take off their heads!

Our world is equally threatening and dangerous. At no time in recent memory has there been more hostility to the Christian faith than there is now. The hatred has reached such a point that one can easily imagine in the near future a law in the Western world that makes it illegal to be a Christian!

What did Daniel and his friends do in their threatening world? They did something that seemed to be so very meagre and unpromising. They prayed!

Centuries later, the people of God would find themselves in a situation much like that which Daniel and his friends were facing. King Herod is on the throne of Israel, and he decides to 'harass' the church (Acts 12:1). He puts James to death, and he throws Simon Peter into prison (12:2–3). It is a dark and ominous time. And what does the church do? Luke tells us: 'constant prayer was offered to God' (12:5).

Here is Herod with all his power and with all sorts of means to work his will. And here is the church resorting to prayer. Prayer seems to be such a pitiful resource in the face of such a monstrous challenge. But we know how the story ends. God owned and used the prayers of his people to completely reverse the situation. The chapter begins with James dying and Herod prevailing. It ends with Herod dying and the Word of God prevailing.

We do not know what we do when we pray! Prayer puts the people of God in touch with God, and with God, nothing at all is impossible.

Many Christians look at our threatening world and they conclude that we must seek political power. We must get organized. We must sign petitions. We must get the right people elected. But the church's great resource is always prayer, and the most important business before the church, other than the preaching of the gospel, is fervent prayer that seeks the face of God.

God's word to his people has not changed: '… if My people who are called by My name will humble themselves, and pray and seek My face, and turn from their wicked ways, then I will hear from heaven, and will forgive their sin and heal their land' (2 Chr. 7:14). With such a promise from God, why is it that we are not praying? It is harder to get the people of God to pray than anything else, and yet the situation in which we find ourselves demands prayer more than anything else.

FOR FURTHER STUDY

1. Read Esther 6. Who is the sleepless king in this passage? What were the consequences of his sleeplessness for Mordecai?

2. Read Genesis 40:1–41:57. How did God use the dreams described here to change Joseph's life?

TO THINK ABOUT AND DISCUSS

1. Are you often tempted to think that God is not at work in this world? Why? What evidence can you see that God is at work?

2. How does this chapter encourage you in your work for the Lord? How does it challenge you, particularly with regard to your attitude to prayer?

Note

1 **Ronald S. Wallace,** *The Message of Daniel* (Bible Speaks Today series; Leicester: Inter-Varsity Press, 1979), p. 52.

4 A statue and a stone

Daniel 2:24–49

The Lord God of heaven answered Daniel's prayer by giving him both the dream of Nebuchadnezzar and its interpretation. After receiving the Lord's answer, Daniel immediately spoke to Arioch, the captain of the guard, saying, 'Do not destroy the wise men of Babylon; take me before the king, and I will tell the king the interpretation' (v. 24).

Once in the presence of the king, Daniel first made clear that the dream and interpretation he was about to give had come from the God of heaven and that he, Daniel, deserved no credit or praise (vv. 28–30). He then proceeded to share both the dream and its interpretation.

THE DREAM

Nebuchadnezzar's dream consisted of a great statue or image. This statue had these distinct features: a head of gold, chest and arms of silver, belly and thighs of bronze, legs of iron and feet of iron and clay (vv. 32–33).

The dream also featured a stone that seemed to come out of nowhere. It struck the statue on the feet, and the whole statue came crashing down (vv. 34–35).

But there was more. As Nebuchadnezzar watched, the little

stone grew and grew until it finally became a great mountain that filled the whole earth (v. 35).

Having stated the dream, Daniel proceeded to give:

THE INTERPRETATION

THE STATUE

Nebuchadnezzar's statue has been interpreted in various ways. Some take a general view of it, arguing that we should not try to associate the various parts of the statue with any particular kingdom. They contend that the statue was intended to convey one truth and one truth only: one kingdom will succeed another until the end of time, at which time there will only be God's kingdom.

Others believe that we can actually identify the four kingdoms. We know that the first was Babylon itself. Daniel explicitly identifies Nebuchadnezzar as the head of gold (vv. 37–38). But Nebuchadnezzar's kingdom, great as it was, would not last. It would be destroyed and replaced by another kingdom. This kingdom would be inferior to Babylon, as silver is inferior to gold. The chest and arms of silver may very well represent the Medo-Persian kingdom which conquered Babylon (v. 39).

That kingdom would also come to an end and be replaced by a third kingdom, represented by the belly and thighs of bronze (v. 39). This is probably a reference to the Grecian Empire which displaced Medo-Persia. It is interesting that this kingdom eventually split into two 'legs'—Syrian and Egyptian.

The fourth kingdom, depicted by the legs of iron and the

feet of iron and clay (vv. 40–43), refers to the Roman Empire, which replaced Greece as the dominant world power. The Roman Empire consisted of two major 'feet', east and west, and, by the way, eventually split into ten smaller kingdoms (represented by the toes).

THE STONE
With this explanation of the statue in place, Daniel turned to explain the stone that Nebuchadnezzar had seen. This stone represented yet another kingdom.

There are several things for us to notice about this kingdom.
- It would be set up during the days of the fourth kingdom (v. 44), that is, during the time of the Roman Empire.
- It would be established by 'the God of heaven' (v. 44).
- It would put an end to all the kingdoms of men and would itself never be destroyed (v. 44). The phrase 'shall not be left to other people' means that it would not be turned over to another kingdom as, for example, the Babylonian Empire was turned over to the Medes and Persians.
- It would be of divine origin. The phrase 'cut out of the mountain without hands' is meant to convey that this kingdom would not be created and governed by human hands.
- It would finally hold universal sway. There is no other conclusion for us to draw in light of Daniel's words: 'the stone that struck the image became a great mountain and filled the whole earth' (v. 35).
- Its fulfilment would not be open to question. The kingdom represented by the stone would most certainly

arise. Daniel said, 'The dream is certain, and its interpretation is sure' (v. 45).

All of this is, of course, a prophecy of the Lord Jesus Christ and his kingdom. He and his kingdom answer to each of the details Daniel provided regarding the stone. First, we know that the Lord Jesus came to this earth during the days of the Roman Empire (Luke 2:1). We also know that, according to his own testimony, he was sent by the God of heaven (John 6:33, 38, 51, 57–58).

Furthermore, his kingdom will put an end to all other kingdoms (Phil. 2:9–11). It will hold universal sway. There is coming a day in which it will be said, 'The kingdoms of this world have become the kingdoms of our Lord and of His Christ, and He shall reign forever and ever!' (Rev. 11:15).

We must also observe that Christ's kingdom is of divine origin. It is not contrived or designed by men, and it is not administered by men.

THE APPLICATION

What are we to take away from Daniel's interpretation of Nebuchadnezzar's vision?

Let us first learn that God is in control of this world and all that goes on in it. We can go even further and declare that all that God is doing in this world is connected with and focused on one thing—establishing the kingdom of Christ.

Sometimes the people of God find themselves distressed and depressed because events seem to be spinning out of control. And we sometimes seem to think that we must sustain the kingdoms of men. We can even give the impression that our nation is more important than the kingdom of Christ. Let

Daniel remind us that all the kingdoms of men—including the USA, UK and so on—are destined to perish. There is only one kingdom that will remain!

I once heard Alistair Begg, pastor of Parkside Church in Cleveland, Ohio, tell a story about a young executive of the BBC suggesting to the Director-General that the BBC no longer allow religious broadcasting. When asked the reason, he spoke along these lines: 'No one believes that stuff any more. People don't go to church. They don't read the Bible. There is no point in the BBC doing anything to perpetuate it.' Upon hearing his words, this Director-General replied, 'The church will stand at the grave of the BBC.'

The other big lesson for us to learn is that we had better come to terms with the kingdom of God now if we have not already done so. The most important question that you can ask yourself was asked by the Roman procurator, Pontius Pilate: 'What then shall I do with Jesus who is called Christ?' (Matt. 27:22).

Here is what the Lord Jesus Christ himself demands of us: that we stop blustering our way through life without regard to him and his claims, that we recognize that he is going to rule over us, and that we submit to his rule even now. He calls upon us to realize that we are not fit to enter his kingdom as we are; that if we are to enter, our sins must be forgiven. And he calls us to embrace what he himself did on the cross as the only possible way that our sins can be forgiven. He assures us that, if we will receive him and the saving benefits of his death, he will indeed receive us as citizens of his kingdom and we will reign with him.

King Nebuchadnezzar, on the other hand, shows us what we are not to do. He realized that he had the correct interpretation of his dream from Daniel and he made sure Daniel was honoured (vv. 46, 48). He also acknowledged that the God of Daniel is the only true God (v. 47), but at this point, he certainly did not embrace the truth of God with his heart. He tipped his hat to the truth and walked away. And he serves as a lasting reminder that a religious experience can stimulate an impressive response at a superficial level and yet leave us untouched in the depths of our hearts.

FOR FURTHER STUDY

1. Read 1 Corinthians 15:24–28. What do these verses teach us about the kingdom of Christ? What will happen to all the kingdoms of the world?
2. Read Revelation 11:15–19. What does the angel announce in these verses? What is the response of the elders?

TO THINK ABOUT AND DISCUSS

1. What does the truth of Christ's kingdom prevailing over all others tell you about how you should conduct your life? How can this truth encourage you when you have to make hard decisions between doing what the world wants you to do and being obedient to God?
2. How should the final triumph of Christ's kingdom mould and shape the way churches go about their ministries? How can it encourage churches when they face opposition?

5 Firm truths from a firm stand

Daniel 3:1–30

As we recall, King Nebuchadnezzar of Babylon had a dream of a statue with a head of gold, arms and chest of silver, belly and thighs of bronze, legs of iron and feet of iron and clay. He asked his wise men to tell him both the dream and its interpretation. They were unable to do so, but Daniel and his friends sought the Lord of heaven, and Daniel was given the answer. The statue represented four kingdoms, and Nebuchadnezzar's kingdom of Babylon was the first. It was the head of gold.

Nebuchadnezzar let that head of gold go to his head! He was so intoxicated with his own importance that he decided to build an image of gold to honour himself. This image, which was ninety feet tall and nine feet wide, was 'set up in the plain of Dura' (v. 1). Nebuchadnezzar wanted to make sure that it was easily seen!

Not content merely to build this image, Nebuchadnezzar decreed that everyone bow down and worship before it at the sound of any kind of music (vv. 4–7).

So Nebuchadnezzar had his image, his decree and his music. He also had something else—his furnace. If anyone refused to obey the decree and bow down to the image, the furnace would come into play (v. 6)!

It all has a very modern ring to it. Many in our society are very interested in doing exactly what Nebuchadnezzar was doing—forcing compliance with their way of thinking. While they fancy themselves to be champions of tolerance, they are actually tyrants. These are the people who have given us the term 'political correctness'. They do not hesitate to express their disdain for evangelical Christianity, which often is out of step with their political agenda. And they have their own furnaces with which to enforce compliance. One is the legal system!

Three men in Nebuchadnezzar's kingdom were not impressed with his image, his decree, his music or his furnace. These were Jerusalem men. Yes, they were living in Babylon, but their values and convictions came from Jerusalem, where they had lived until Nebuchadnezzar's army snatched them away. Filled with the God of Jerusalem, these men could not bow to the king of Babylon.

We have met these young men, Shadrach, Meshach and Abed-Nego, earlier in the book of Daniel (1:7, 11, 17–19; 2:17). Where is Daniel in this episode? We can safely assume that he was out of the country. He had by this time risen to a position of such prominence that it would not be unusual at all for him to be representing the king in other countries. We still need to include this chapter in our study because, while Daniel himself was absent, his spirit, the Jerusalem spirit, was certainly present.

THE MOMENT OF TRUTH

It was only a matter of time before Shadrach, Meshach and Abed-Nego ran afoul of the king's decree. The inevitable day arrived. The three men were present when the music played and they refused to bow. There was no way for them to go unnoticed. They were standing on ground that was as flat as a pancake, and everyone around them bowed. I cannot help but wonder if these three men also turned towards Jerusalem while they were standing on the plain of Babylon!

They could have rationalized the situation. They could have said, 'After all, it is just a cultural courtesy. It is just a matter of giving Nebuchadnezzar his due. And he really is a great man. So we can bow to his image, but still worship the real God in our hearts.' But Shadrach, Meshach and Abed-Nego would not bow! They were painfully aware that they were there in Babylon because their people had played fast and loose with God's laws. They were there primarily because their people had been especially careless about the first two commandments. Armed with that knowledge, they refused to compromise. Faced with the moment of truth, they had truth for the moment. And the truth they had consisted of the commandments of God.

After all the bowing was over, some of the Babylonian officials scrambled to their feet and ran to King Nebuchadnezzar. They were eager to report Shadrach, Meshach and Abed-Nego! Listen to the words these officials spoke to the king: 'There are certain Jews whom you have set over the affairs of the province of Babylon: Shadrach, Meshach, and Abed-Nego; these men, O king, have not paid due regard to you. They do not serve your gods or worship the gold image which you have set up' (v. 12).

Their words tell us a couple of things about these officials. First, they disliked Shadrach, Meshach and Abed-Nego simply because they were Jews. Listen to how they spit out the words 'certain Jews'! Second, they disliked these men because Nebuchadnezzar had given them authority.

The disobedience of Meshach, Shadrach and Abed-Nego enraged Nebuchadnezzar, but he decided to give them another opportunity to prove themselves good Babylonians (v. 15). But Shadrach, Meshach and Abed-Nego did not need it. Their decision not to bow was based on firm and settled convictions that would not change. It was not due to a momentary fit of stubbornness or a temporary lapse of judgement!

So all that was left was the furnace, and, in a fit of unmatched fury, Nebuchadnezzar commanded that it be heated seven times more than usual (v. 19) and the three young men thrown in. On this occasion, God chose to deliver his people, and he did so in a most striking and marvellous way: by sending a fourth man into the fire to protect them (v. 25). We should not be in doubt about the identity of this man. It was none other than the Lord Jesus Christ himself in one of his pre-incarnate appearances. And he so protected his servants that they emerged from the furnace without so much as the smell of smoke (v. 27)!

TRUTH FOR OUR MOMENT

THE TRUTH ABOUT DUTY

Shadrach, Meshach and Abed-Nego did not know whether God would deliver them from the fiery furnace. But they did know that they could not bow to Nebuchadnezzar's image (vv. 16–18). Stuart Olyott draws from them this lesson: 'Our duty, and the limit of our duty, is to do what is right. That is it. There is nothing more. If doing right means that we are ruined, that is

God's affair. Consequences are in His hands, but duty is in ours. Our job in life is to do what pleases Him, whatever the cost, and whatever the outcome.'[1]

Are you wondering what you would do if you were in that situation? Many of us have the answer. We are bowing right now! Babylon is playing its music, and we are bowing! We already think, act, talk and dress like the Babylonians!

THE TRUTH ABOUT GOD'S PRESENCE

We can be confident that the news of Meshach, Shadrach and Abed-Nego travelled rapidly among the Jewish captives in Babylon. We can also be confident that they drew from that news tremendous consolation. All the Jews in Babylon were in something of a furnace themselves: a furnace of affliction! The experience of their three fellow-Jews enabled them to conclude two things: the Lord himself would be with them in that furnace of affliction, and in due time he would deliver them, just as he had Meshach, Shadrach and Abed-Nego.

As we face our own trials and afflictions, let us draw the same conclusion.

THE TRUTH ABOUT GOD'S SOVEREIGNTY

We are mistaken to conclude from this passage that God will deliver his people from every circumstance that they find difficult or unpleasant. God chose on this occasion to deliver Meshach, Shadrach and Abed-Nego. At other times, he lets his people die. In Acts 12, Peter is miraculously delivered, but James is killed. Why the difference? The answer is locked up in the counsels of God who works all things according to his will. It is our job to trust him, not to decipher his workings.

THE TRUTH ABOUT ETERNAL SALVATION

The experience of Shadrach, Meshach and Abed-Nego pictures a reality that each and every Christian has experienced. The Bible tells us that we come into this world with a sinful nature that causes us to be under the sentence of God's wrath. Because of sin, we are all destined to go into the furnace of eternal destruction.

But the Lord Jesus came into that furnace! He did so on the cross. There he experienced the wrath of God, and all who believe in him will never have to experience that wrath themselves. He came into my furnace so I could come out unharmed! Geoff Thomas writes,

… what do we see when we flood this passage with the light of Calvary? Don't we see the Son of God in the furnace? Do our minds turn to Golgotha? Do we think of how the Lord Jesus Christ, in visiting us, entered the lake of fire there for us? The flames of hell can never go out, but the Lord Christ voluntarily enters into Calvary's hell for us, that we might walk the cool glades of heaven in peace with him, upon the green pastures and by its still waters for ever and ever.[2]

For further study ▶

FOR FURTHER STUDY

1. Read Esther 3:8. What reason did Haman give the king for his hatred of the Jews?
2. Read John 15:18–25. What did Jesus tell his disciples to expect in this world, and why?

TO THINK ABOUT AND DISCUSS

1. How do you explain the intense dislike so many have for Christians? Have you experienced something of this in your own life?
2. How does the world today pressure God's people to comply? Think of government legislation, peer pressure and so on.

Notes

1 **Olyott,** p. 44.
2 **Thomas,** p. 39.

6 Jerusalem grace in a Babylon heart

Daniel 4:1–37

In this chapter and in chapters 7 through 9, our focus will be on two of Babylon's kings, Nebuchadnezzar and Belshazzar. While lingering to some degree in the background, Daniel was always ready, as we shall see in the case of Belshazzar, to step forward and faithfully represent the God of Jerusalem.

We have been thinking about Daniel and his friends maintaining Jerusalem values while they were living in Babylon. Jerusalem was far more than a place to these men. It represented a set of beliefs and values that were entirely different from those of Babylon. In particular, Jerusalem represented the grace of God coming into the human realm to make people his own and to so change and thrill them that they desired to live according to his laws and for his glory. Jerusalem was all about God, while Babylon was all about man.

This chapter brings us to a most wonderful and cheering truth. It is the testimony of King Nebuchadnezzar regarding his conversion to the true knowledge of the true God. The same grace that had worked in Jerusalem is not restricted to Jerusalem. It now invades Babylon to win the heart of her king!

As we examine Nebuchadnezzar's account of his

conversion, we are able to identify three distinct stages. Each of these stages is present in every instance of true conversion.

NEBUCHADNEZZAR AT REST

After some words of introduction (vv. 1–3), Nebuchadnezzar takes up his story with these words: 'I, Nebuchadnezzar, was at rest in my house, and flourishing in my palace.'

We know about Nebuchadnezzar. As the king of the world's greatest power of that era, he was full of himself. Daniel 3 shows us that! Although several evidences for God had come his way, Nebuchadnezzar had never truly come to faith in God. He had dismissed the evidences, and God was far from his thoughts.

We may believe that we have nothing in common with one so great as Nebuchadnezzar. We are not kings of great empires! The truth, however, is that we have a lot more in common with this man than we might suppose! Made by God for the purposes of knowing God and living for his glory, we, like Nebuchadnezzar, refuse to do so. As he did with Nebuchadnezzar, God has put several reminders in our way that we should be living for him, but, like Nebuchadnezzar, we have dismissed those evidences, living as if God is not even there!

We are like Nebuchadnezzar. Full of ourselves! Going about our business! Completely at peace with ourselves when we should be disturbed about the condition and destiny of our souls!

But Nebuchadnezzar was not allowed to continue in his self-satisfied, tranquil state. The next thing we see is:

NEBUCHADNEZZAR DISTURBED

Nebuchadnezzar writes, 'I saw a dream which made me afraid, and the thoughts on my bed and the visions of my head troubled me' (v. 5). He had been down this path before! A dream troubled him! As before, he brought in his 'wise men' (v. 7), and they were once again unable to help him.

So Nebuchadnezzar did what he should have done from the start. He called for Daniel (vv. 8–9) and related to him his dream.

This dream consisted of a very tall and strong tree standing in the midst of the earth. It was so tall that 'Its height reached to the heavens' (v. 11). Furthermore, its leaves were lovely and its fruit abundant (v. 12).

This begins as a most pleasant dream. But things rapidly change! One whom Nebuchadnezzar identifies as 'a watcher' appears and cries, 'Chop down the tree and cut off its branches' (vv. 13–14)!

This is God stepping into Nebuchadnezzar's comfortable and easy life! God steps in by sending one of his angels to announce that Nebuchadnezzar's life is not going to go on as it had up to that point.

How urgently the message of this angel is needed today! Most people are going about their lives as if their lives will never change. They are living as if they will never have to die and face eternity! They are living as if they will always have their cars, computers, cellphones and televisions. They are living as if they will always have their vacations, their ball games and their money.

But it is all going to come to a screeching halt some day! And the question that begs to be answered is this: what then? But most people never give the slightest impression of ever having thought about that question for as much as a single moment!

The tree in his dream represented Nebuchadnezzar himself. He was the great, majestic and beautiful tree. But a decree had gone out from heaven regarding him, and that decree essentially consisted of these words: 'Chop down that tree!' (see v. 14).

We may be thinking that this has nothing to do with us. This had to do with Nebuchadnezzar, not with us! If that is our thinking, we need to think again! The Lord Jesus told a parable about a man who planted a fig-tree. He did so with the expectation that it would bear figs. But when the time came for it to have figs, there were none. When his patience was exhausted, the man said to the keeper of his vineyard, 'Cut it down; why does it use up the ground?' (Luke 13:6–9). The context of the parable makes it clear that the Lord Jesus was speaking to people in general about the need to get right with God. This parable was meant to drive the message home to people in general! It applies to us! God has planted each and every one of us with the expectation of getting something from our lives! And we have not given him anything! And we think that we will be able to go right on living as we always have. We think we can go on ignoring the God who has made us and who has the right to expect fruit from our lives. But we are deluded. A decree has gone out from heaven regarding every single person who lives with no thought of God, and that decree is the same as it was for Nebuchadnezzar. That decree says, 'Cut that tree down!'

A time of being cut down is coming for each and every one of us! Do you think about this? Are you ready for it? Are you prepared for life to end? Are you prepared to face God and eternity?

Sometimes the cutting down does not mean death. That will be the final expression of it. But it can also refer to any trouble that comes in to disrupt and disturb our lives. The cutting down of Nebuchadnezzar would consist of him suffering from a disease (lycanthropy) that would make him think and act like an animal (vv. 14–16).

Let us never doubt that God has no shortage of ways of getting our attention! The decree announced by the angel came true. A year passed, and Nebuchadnezzar probably assured himself that nothing was going to happen, but he was suddenly stricken and for a period of 'seven times' (v. 16) he was like a beast of the field.

Some have heard the warnings of God about judgement to come and they have trembled, but day followed day and week followed week, and their trembling stopped as they fell right back into their comfortable living without regard to God. But God's delays should never be taken to mean that his promises will not be carried out!

That brings us to the third and final instalment of Nebuchadnezzar's experience:

NEBUCHADNEZZAR CHANGED

The mercy of God was great towards Nebuchadnezzar. It was a mercy that God gave him the dream. It was a mercy that God gave him the interpretation. It was a mercy that God gave him a year to prepare. Yes, it was even a mercy that God made him like a beast for a period. And it was a mercy that God restored to the man his understanding (v. 34).

What do you think? Having drunk so deeply from the well of mercy, do you think it was possible for Nebuchadnezzar to go right back to what he was before? No! God's mercies had all been designed for a purpose, as the 'holy one ... from heaven' so clearly stated: '... in order that the living may know that the Most High rules in the kingdom of men ...' (v. 17).

Do you understand this? Do you understand that heaven rules? It doesn't often seem so. Many are living as if money rules. Many are living as if pleasure rules. Many are living as if family and friends rule. Many are living as if the latest fad rules. Many are living as if their careers rule. But these are all delusions hatched by the devil and sent out of the gates of hell, the very place to which all who fall for them must finally go!

Heaven rules! And when that great, final day of 'cutting down' comes, we will know it very well. Then those who have lived for their trinkets and pleasures will cry for the mountains and rocks to fall upon them, because that is a lesser disaster than standing unprepared in the presence of the holy God!

But those who have prepared for eternity by taking refuge in Jesus will stand in that same day with confidence and assurance. The rule of heaven, which terrifies sinners, will be the delight and joy of their redeemed hearts.

FOR FURTHER STUDY

1. Read Matthew 16:26. How much importance does Jesus attach to salvation? What are the greatest things that this world can offer, and what is their ultimate value?

2. Read Acts 9:1–9. Whose conversion is described in these verses? What truths about conversion can you draw from this account?

TO THINK ABOUT AND DISCUSS

1. How do you respond to the account of Nebuchadnezzar's conversion? How can such an account bring encouragement to us?

2. List some other notable conversion stories in history. Think of people in the Bible, such as the apostle Paul, as well as people who have lived more recently. What do such conversions show us about God and how he works?

7 What sinners cannot do

Daniel 5:1–9

This chapter brings us to a new king in Babylon. As a matter of fact, Babylon had two kings at this time. The king in this passage, Belshazzar, was co-regent with his father, Nabonidus.

These were serious times in Babylon. The once-mighty empire was being threatened by a new power—the Medes and Persians. The threat was so very great that Nabonidus was leading his army into battle at the very same time that Belshazzar was throwing the wild party described in these verses! Here is an amazing thing: a king partying while disaster looms! It is not hard to see in this a picture of many today. Western nations continue to creak and wobble under the weight of years of indulging ourselves and thumbing our noses at God. Disaster is approaching! But most party on!

Why did the Spirit of God see fit to include in Scripture this account of a pagan king and a drunken orgy? I suggest that it was because there is in Belshazzar a picture of every person who is apart from God. Belshazzar would die before the night described in this chapter was over, but in a very real sense he lives on in each and every person who refuses to submit to God.

Belshazzar is every sinner! As we look at sinners in general, we are able to see certain things that they cannot do.

THEY CANNOT JUST IGNORE GOD

When Belshazzar decided to have his party, he could not be content just to drink his wine with his friends; he must have his friends drink from the gold and silver vessels that Nebuchadnezzar had seized when he destroyed the temple in Jerusalem (v. 2).

This is a remarkable thing! The Babylonians had conquered many countries, and in the process of that conquering they had seized many sacred vessels from many sacred houses. Have you ever wondered why Belshazzar specified that the sacred vessels from Jerusalem be used? Why these vessels alone?

It seems that Belshazzar knew that the God of Jerusalem was not in the same category as the gods of other nations. It was as if he could not get this God out of his mind. This God bugged him! This God had to be discredited! This God had to be treated with contempt!

The thing that drove Belshazzar is still driving people today. Why is it that unbelievers feel the need to attack the God of the Bible? Why do they want to take his name in vain? When was the last time you heard the adherent of a non-Christian religion take the name of his or her god in vain? But you hear the Lord's name used carelessly in this way several times a day!

Why is the God of Christianity singled out for contempt and disdain? Why don't unbelievers just ignore God? Why do they feel compelled constantly to offer their opinions on God and on the various teachings of the Bible?

The very fact that sinners cannot ignore God is proof that they intuitively know that he exists and that they are accountable to him. In belittling and ridiculing God they are in fact proving him. They are deliberately trying to suppress knowledge that will not entirely go away.

THEY CANNOT ACCEPT THE EVIDENCE FOR GOD

Belshazzar had plenty of evidence for the God of Jerusalem. He knew about Daniel's interpretations of Nebuchadnezzar's dreams. He knew about the fiery furnace and about the conversion of Nebuchadnezzar.

The evidence spoke very powerfully of the absolute supremacy of the God of Jerusalem and the need for everyone to bow in submission to him. But Belshazzar did not like where the evidence led. To accept the evidence would mean going in a direction he did not want to go in. It would mean that his life would be changed. It would mean that he would have to break with his darling sins. Unable to tolerate all that the evidence demanded, Belshazzar chose to ignore the evidence. He put himself in the peculiar position of treating with contempt the supreme God who demanded his submission.

Many are in that same odd position. God has given us all kinds of evidence for receiving Jesus as our Lord and Saviour. The miracles he performed, the teachings he offered, the changed lives of those who followed him, his resurrection—all of these are powerful and convincing proofs of the need to bow in submission to Christ. But many are doing as Belshazzar did—treating with contempt the very one before whom they should bow. We could call it 'the Belshazzar syndrome'.

THEY CANNOT KEEP CREATED THINGS IN THEIR PROPER PLACE

In light of the evidence, it is astonishing that Belshazzar refused to worship the God of heaven. It is even more astonishing that he chose to worship 'the gods of gold and silver, bronze and iron, wood and stone' (v. 4).

There is nothing wrong with any of these materials. God made them all! The wrong comes in elevating the things that God has created above God himself.

It sounds silly to put created things above the one who created them. The Creator is obviously greater than the created! But Belshazzar did, and we continue to do the same thing. When we put our families, our possessions, our games above God, we are repeating the error of Belshazzar. We would do well to heed these words from the apostle Paul: 'Set your mind on things above, not on things on the earth' (Col. 3:2).

THEY CANNOT KEEP GOD FROM JUDGING

Belshazzar could treat the sacred vessels with contempt. He could place created things above the Creator. But he could not dethrone or destroy God. God does not go away because people do not believe in him. He does not vacate his throne because people treat him with contempt.

Belshazzar learned this in a most dreadful and frightening way. In the midst of his drunken revelry 'the fingers of a man's hand appeared and wrote opposite the lampstand on the plaster of the wall of the king's palace ... ' (v. 5). That hand was the hand of God and it wrote about the judgement that was soon to fall. Belshazzar thought he was getting away with his disdain for God, but he had seriously miscalculated. The God who gives us the strength and energy to sin will eventually call us to account for our sins. We can get away with our sins for a while, but we should never take God's delaying judgement to mean that there will be no judgement. It will come in God's own time and way.

The apostle Paul writes, 'So then each of us shall give account of himself to God' (Rom. 14:12). And the author of Hebrews adds, '… it is appointed for men to die once, but after this the judgment … ' (Heb. 9:27). Stuart Olyott puts it like this: 'Who knows when God will say to a person, "One more sin will be your last." Then the writing will be on the wall for you.'[1]

Mark this down—no one will get to heaven without his or her sin being judged. God judges sin in one of two ways: either in the sinner, or in one who stands as a substitute for the sinner. In all of history, there is only one who can serve as a substitute for sinners. That is Jesus. He can do so because he has no sin of his own.

That is the reason why he went to the cross. There he endured the penalty of God's wrath for all who will believe in him. Because he endured it, there is no wrath left for those sinners who rest themselves on what he did.

But if our sin is not judged in Jesus, we must endure the penalty of it ourselves. And that means that we, in the words of the apostle Paul, 'shall be punished with everlasting destruction from the presence of the Lord and from the glory of His power …' (2 Thes. 1:9).

We can go through life mocking God and treating him with contempt, as Belshazzar did, but we cannot finally escape him. We must come before him either bearing our own sins or taking refuge in the Jesus who bore them in our stead.

How do we take refuge in Jesus? We do so by honestly facing up to our sins and asking God to forgive us on the basis of what Jesus did.

FOR FURTHER STUDY

1. Read 2 Corinthians 4:3–6. How does Paul describe unbelievers? What needs to happen for unbelievers to come out of their darkness?
2. Read Revelation 20:11–15. What do these verses teach about God's judgement?

TO THINK ABOUT AND DISCUSS

1. On the basis of your conversations with unbelieving friends and family members, what do you find to be their objections to Christianity? Are there ways in which you can help counter these objections—for example, through discussion or simply living a godly life?
2. How do you explain the inability of sinners to ignore God? Have you experienced something of this yourself, either before you became a Christian or perhaps since then, during a time of backsliding?

Note

1 **Olyott,** p. 73.

8 Dying to have a good time

Daniel 5:10–31

Is it possible to find a sadder passage of Scripture? Here Belshazzar, king of Babylon, throws a wild, drunken party with the army of the Medes and Persians poised to conquer the city. A carousing king in a collapsing city!

It gives us a picture of our own age. There are all kinds of indications that our society is marching towards collapse. We know for sure that those who have no regard for God are headed for a very great collapse indeed. But the motto of many is 'Party on!' It may very well be that our time will go down in history as 'the party era'.

Belshazzar was jolted from his drunken stupor by the sudden appearance of some fingers that wrote these words on the wall: 'MENE, MENE, TEKEL, UPHARSIN' (v. 25).

His wise men could not interpret these words, but, at his mother's suggestion, Daniel was brought in. And Daniel gave the king the meaning of each word. 'MENE' meant 'numbered'; 'TEKEL' meant 'weighed'; and 'UPHARSIN' meant 'divided'. Belshazzar's number was up. He had been weighed in God's balance and found wanting. Now his kingdom was to be divided or destroyed.

The ancient king of a collapsing kingdom: what does it have to do with us? The answer is plain. We are dealing with the

FACE2FACE: DANIEL

very same God as was Belshazzar, and this God is still the numberer, the weigher and the destroyer.

GOD IS THE NUMBERER

Just as Belshazzar's days were numbered, so are ours. Most people seem to live as if this life is going to go on for ever. They will always have their gadgets, their pleasures and, yes, their parties. Even though death constantly parades itself before our eyes, multitudes of people seem to ignore it. As if that will make it go away!

Meanwhile, the Bible solemnly testifies to the shortness of this life and the steady, unrelenting approach of death. The author of Hebrews tells us that we each have an appointment with death (Heb. 9:27). Ours is a day in which many people are quite careless about their appointments, but this is one appointment that everyone will keep!

The Bible also tells us that our times are in the Lord's hands. The truth of the matter is that God has set an exact time for each of us to live, and no one can change either the day or the hour.

How very wise we are if we live with the awareness that death is coming! How very foolish we are if we live without that awareness! The rich farmer of Luke 12 ordered his life without regard to death, but that did not keep death from coming! And when it came, it found him unprepared. The solemn epitaph that Jesus pronounced on this man consists of one word: 'Fool!' (Luke 12:20).

GOD IS THE WEIGHER

This life is much more than merely waiting for death; this life is a testing time. It is a weighing time, and God is the one who is doing the weighing.

Belshazzar did not realize it, but he had been in God's scales all along. When Daniel arrived on the scene, he made this very clear to Belshazzar.

Perhaps Belshazzar thought that it was only his business how he lived. A lot of people have been heard to say, 'It's my life, and how I live it is my business!' But Daniel showed Belshazzar that life was not just his business, it was also God's business. Daniel put it this way: '… the God who holds your breath in His hand and owns all your ways, you have not glorified' (v. 23b).

In Daniel's words we have the purpose for which God has given us life. We are his creatures, and we are made to live for his glory. It is not your life to live for your pleasure; it is rather life from God to live for his pleasure!

Belshazzar knew this from the reign of Nebuchadnezzar (v. 22), who was probably his grandfather (the word translated 'father' in v. 18 is often used in the Bible to refer to any ancestor). God had given Nebuchadnezzar his life, his power, his prestige. It all came from God! But Nebuchadnezzar refused to acknowledge God. He allowed his heart to be lifted up with pride, as if he were responsible for everything that he enjoyed! And when his heart was lifted up with pride, God humbled him until he finally came to acknowledge God (vv. 18–21).

Belshazzar should have learned from this, but he didn't. He rather allowed the very same pride that gripped Nebuchadnezzar to grip him. He 'lifted' himself 'up against the Lord of heaven' (v. 23). What folly it was for him to do so!

FACE2FACE: DANIEL

A weak, puny man lifting himself up against the very God who was holding his breath (v. 23)!

Stuart Olyott puts Daniel's message to Belshazzar in these words:

Your secret sins and open sins, your misspent hours, your cruelty, pride, wild disorders, and drunkenness, your neglect of holy things and your spiritual resistance—God has weighed it all up. Each one has gone into His balance. He has considered your life from beginning to end, and it does not come up to the mark. It does not satisfy His standards.[1]

God had weighed Belshazzar and had found him lacking! The same God is weighing each of us. What is he saying about you and your life right now? He put you here to live for his glory. Are you doing it?

What does it mean to live for God's glory? It means to live in the way in which he wants us to live. It is to live according to his commands. It is to live in such a way that we reflect God and give others a good impression of him.

We have plenty of reasons to live for God's glory. He gives us the very air we breathe (v. 23). He 'owns' all our ways (v. 23). All of our ability to think and do comes from God. Every single thought and every single act is either caused or permitted by him. Nothing in our lives falls outside the sovereignty of God.

Since we owe our lives, and everything in them, to God, it should be our desire to live for his glory! But, sinners that we are, we take what God has given us for ourselves. We use his very gifts to thumb our noses in his face.

Because God is patient, we get by for a while without living for him. We can get by with it for so long that we fondly imagine that we will never have to give account of ourselves. But the God who is weighing our every thought, deed and word is finally going to bring us before his judgement bar (Rom. 14:12; Heb. 9:27). At that time, those who have mocked his name, violated his commands and scorned his ways will see God in yet another light.

GOD IS THE DESTROYER
The night in which God wrote on Belshazzar's wall was also the night of Belshazzar's destruction. The God who had numbered his days and weighed his actions also brought an end to him.

That very night the Medes and Persians, under Darius, conquered the city of Babylon and put Belshazzar to death. We might say that God shut out the lights and the party was over! But the tragedy of Belshazzar goes far beyond him losing his own kingdom. He lost a far greater kingdom—the kingdom of God! Belshazzar held God in contempt, and God destroyed him!

People do not like to hear God called a destroyer. As far as we are concerned, God is a kindly old grandfather who expresses disappointment with the way we live but never does anything more! That is the God of the latest opinion polls; he is not the God of the Bible. The Bible tells us that the true God is 'a consuming fire' (Heb. 12:29). The Lord Jesus himself said of God, 'Fear Him who, after He has killed, has power to cast into hell; yes, I say to you, fear Him!' (Luke 12:5).

Does it sound unreasonable to say that God is a destroying

God? Ask yourself what you would do if you were to make something for a specific purpose and it did not work. You would destroy it! It is the same with God. He has made us for a specific purpose—to live for his glory. If we do not do so, he will destroy us!

The truth is that we all share Belshazzar's indictment. We have all refused to live for the glory of God (Rom. 3:23). The good news is that we don't have to share Belshazzar's ruin. The God whom we have offended has graciously made a way for our sins to be forgiven. That way is his Son, Jesus Christ. The Lord Jesus lived the life that we have refused to live. He brought glory to God in everything he thought, said and did. And then he went to the cross to pay the penalty that sinners deserve for not living for the glory of God.

Those who come to God sincerely acknowledging their refusal to live for his glory and deeply repenting of the same will find free and warm forgiveness on the basis of what Jesus did.

For further study ▶

FOR FURTHER STUDY

1. Read 2 Chronicles 33:10–13, 21–23. What kings are named in these verses? What did one do that the other refused to do?
2. Read Psalms 7:11–13; 21:8–12; 145:20. What do these verses tell us about God and the wicked?

TO THINK ABOUT AND DISCUSS

1. How do you respond to the thought of God being the numberer, weigher and destroyer? How do you explain the fact that these truths are so seldom emphasized?
2. What can you do to encourage your pastor and your church to emphasize God as the numberer, weigher and destroyer?

Note

1 **Olyott,** p. 71.

9 The nub of it all

Daniel 5:23

We return one more time to the account of Belshazzar to take note of this single verse. We do so because it so perfectly captures and expresses the situation of every person in this world. Although Belshazzar was king of an empire, he is in a very real sense a representative man. He represents all who are still in their sins and apart from God.

We do not have to be kings who give ourselves over to drunken revelry to find ourselves in Belshazzar. We don't have to drink wine from sacred vessels from Jerusalem to find ourselves in this man. We do not have to die at the hands of Medes and Persians to be inexorably linked to him.

Our text is the key to discovering the link between Belshazzar and ourselves. I do not know of a more powerful and revealing statement in the Bible.

First, this verse shows us:

WHAT GOD DEMANDS

Why are we here? We could easily get the impression from observing others that we are here merely to consume. We are here to eat, drink and enjoy the various pleasures that life has to offer. But this verse shows us something quite different. We are here because we were made by God and for God.

God made us for the purpose of bringing glory to his name. We are here to live for his honour and his praise. We are to live in such a way that we reflect God and reflect that it is a joy and privilege to live for him. We are to live in such a way that others can see that God makes us happy.

Doesn't it make sense to live in this way? God is the one who has given us life. God is the one who has sustained our lives to this present moment. He is the one who has heaped blessing after blessing upon us. We all have our burdens and our difficulties, but with them all we have to say that we have been given many good things to enjoy. The Bible will leave us no room to wiggle on this point. If we call anything good, we have to say it came to us from God (James 1:17).

We have, then, plenty of incentives for living for the glory of God. But how are we to go about doing this? It is one thing to say that we are to live for God's glory, but quite another to know how to proceed.

The Bible is clear on this as well. It does not allow us to define for ourselves what it means to live for the glory of God. No, it is far more precise than that! To live for God's glory is to live according to his commandments. A lot of people assure themselves that they are living for the honour of God because they define it in a way that they find comfortable.

But here is how God defines it:
- we are to have no other gods before him;
- we are not to use any man-made devices in worshipping him;
- we are not to take his name in vain;
- we are not to use his day as if it were our own day or as if it were just like any other day;

- we are to honour our parents;
- we are not to murder, commit adultery, steal, lie or covet.

This is how God tells us to live! And living this way honours him! This is the purpose for which Belshazzar was made, and it is the same purpose for which we are made.

That brings us to our second consideration:

HOW WE HAVE PERFORMED

Belshazzar was made to live for God, but here is the solemn and terrifying indictment that came from God: 'the God who holds your breath in His hand and owns all your ways, you have not glorified.'

We are mistaken if we read this only as God's verdict on Belshazzar. It is his verdict on every single person who has ever lived with the sole exception of the Lord Jesus Christ.

As we have noted, living for the glory of God is a matter of living in conformity with his laws. Belshazzar had refused to do so, choosing rather to thumb his nose in God's face.

Perhaps you are saying that you are not as bad as all that. You are not doing as Belshazzar did! But look at God's laws. Are you keeping them? Are you putting him first, or are you constantly putting other things ahead of him? How are you doing with his name? Are you always treating it with respect, using it only with reverence? How are you doing with his day? Are you honouring it? Perhaps you are saying that you haven't murdered anybody! But do you hate anyone?

You may not feel like a sinner, but it is not a matter of your feeling. If your doctor says that you have a life-threatening illness, you may be shocked because you feel well. But doctors have certain objective tests. They have their scans and their blood work, and these objective tests spell out the truth.

So it is with us. God has his law, and that law indicts us no matter how we feel! No one can stand before the law of God and claim to have perfectly kept it. No one can stand before it and profess to be living for the glory of God. That is why we have the apostle Paul emphatically saying, 'all have sinned and fall short of the glory of God' (Rom. 3:23).

The truth of it is that God has put all of us in his scales, just as he did Belshazzar. On the right side, he puts in a weight which we can call the glory of God. And in we go on the left side. And immediately the right side drops to its lowest point, and we, in the left scale, are hoisted in the air. When it comes to measuring up to the law of God, we have no weight! And God is taking it all in. The God who made us is the God who measures us, and having done so, he pronounces the very same conclusion as he did with Belshazzar: 'You have been weighed in the balances, and found wanting' (v. 27).

That very night Belshazzar lost his life, but that was a much smaller loss than the other he experienced, namely eternal acceptance with God. How do we know that Belshazzar lost that? The Bible thunderously answers, 'The wicked shall be turned into hell, and all the nations that forget God' (Ps. 9:17).

Is there any hope, then? What can those do who have become keenly aware of God's high standard and their own low performance? The answer is only indirectly given in the account of Belshazzar. When Daniel was brought in to interpret the handwriting on the wall, he said, 'you ... Belshazzar, have not humbled your heart, although you knew ...' (v. 22). Daniel was talking about God's dealings with

Belshazzar's grandfather, King Nebuchadnezzar. Belshazzar knew about these dealings (v. 22). He knew that God had dealt with his grandfather in such a way that Nebuchadnezzar was convinced of the reality of God and humbled himself.

And this is what God requires of us all. He has given us all kinds of evidence for his truth, and he now requires that we humble ourselves and accept it, that we stop marching through life as if we know it all and as if God is nowhere to be found. He demands that we recognize God as God, recognize ourselves as his creatures and recognize that our only hope lies in humbling ourselves before him.

God sent his Son into this world to live in perfect obedience to the law which we have refused to honour. And then God nailed him to the cross, where he received the wrath that sinners deserve for breaking that law.

Now God says that there is forgiveness for all who will own up to their law-breaking refusal to live for the glory of God. There is forgiveness because of what Jesus did for sinners on the cross.

Now, what will you do? Will you humble yourself and receive that man dying on that cross? It is such a ludicrous and absurd thing: a man dying on a Roman cross outside Jerusalem two thousand years ago! But God unrelentingly points to that man and that cross and says, 'That is my way of salvation!'

We can scorn that cross and ridicule the teaching that it is the way of salvation. But as long as we are scorning and ridiculing, we are not humbling ourselves, and there is no salvation for us until we admit the truth of that cross and humble ourselves.

Our lives have been found wanting! But Jesus is the

sufficient Saviour! The business before us is to face the truth and receive the Saviour.

FOR FURTHER STUDY

1. Read Romans 11:36 and Revelation 4:11. What do these verses teach us about the reason why we were created?
2. Read Romans 1:20–23. What does the apostle Paul tell us about ourselves in relationship to the purpose for which we were created?

TO THINK ABOUT AND DISCUSS

1. What do you think it means to live for God's glory? How should living for God's glory affect the daily decisions we make (for example, about use of time or money), and our relationships with others?
2. What evidence do you see in the world today that most people are not living for the glory of God? Examine your own heart: are you truly living for God's glory?

10 The power and peril of excellence

Daniel 6:1–9

The great empire of Babylon is now no more. It seemed at one time that she was invincible, but the God who sets up kingdoms and takes them down has removed Babylon from the stage of human history and replaced her with the Persian Empire.

Darius the Mede is the first king of this fledgling kingdom. As this chapter opens, we find him trying to get a handle on things. He decides to do so by setting 120 'satraps' (protectors) over his kingdom (v. 1). These satraps are to be under the oversight of three governors, who will in turn report directly to Darius himself.

Darius had not been in charge long before he discovered that he had a very valuable and precious treasure indeed in the form of Daniel. Just how he came to know Daniel is not explained. Suffice it to say that the man who always distinguished himself in Babylon had done so again under Darius.

Darius decided to take advantage of Daniel's unusual abilities by appointing him one of the three governors. But it wasn't long before Darius was so impressed with the man that he was giving thought to making him the prime minister of the whole kingdom (v. 3).

This particular slice of Daniel's life speaks to us about

matters of utmost importance, namely the power and peril of excellence.

THE POWER OF EXCELLENCE

Our passage does not leave us in doubt about the reason why King Darius was so impressed with Daniel. It plainly says of Daniel, 'an excellent spirit was in him' (v. 3).

What are we to understand from this? What is an 'excellent spirit'? The word translated 'excellent' means 'surpassing' or 'excelling'. Daniel had a spirit that went beyond the spirits of others and beyond what others expected to find in him.

We know those things that typify the human spirit. The human spirit is easily offended by the perceived or real faults of others. Once offended, it is very slow to let go of the offence and to forgive.

The human spirit is inclined to be slothful and lazy, to always take the easy way out. It is forever thinking about its own comfort and convenience.

The human spirit is inclined to chafe under the commandments of God. It makes us resent those commandments and go around them. It causes us to rationalize when we have gone around them.

The human spirit causes us to complain when our circumstances are difficult and harsh, to act as if God has been unkind or cruel to us and as if we deserve better.

If we have a clear view of the typical human spirit, we are in a position to understand Daniel's spirit. Daniel went beyond the typical!

Take the matter of his circumstances. He had every reason, it would seem, to be bitter and resentful and to feel as if God had failed him. But Daniel went beyond that. Even though he was taken captive by the Babylonians, Daniel did not allow bitterness about his circumstances to dominate him. He did not allow it to make him angry with God. If God had chosen to take him out of Jerusalem, Daniel would serve him in Babylon!

And serve he did! He gave the very best that he had to offer all the many years that he was in Babylon. He could have harboured such hatred towards his captors that he determined he would do anything and everything except be cooperative. But he saw Babylon as an opportunity to glorify God, to demonstrate the Jerusalem spirit.

We cannot consider the excellent spirit in Daniel without asking ourselves what kind of spirit we are manifesting. We Christians claim to be different from unbelievers. We claim to be new creatures in Christ (2 Cor. 5:17). No, we do not claim to be perfect, but we do claim to be different.

Are we reflecting that difference? Do we have a spirit that goes beyond the typical human spirit? Are we easily offended? Do we hold on to slights and offences, refusing to forgive? Are we slothful and lazy, or are we giving the very best we have to offer? Are we obeying the commandments of God, and glorifying God as we do so because he has given us those commandments? Are we satisfied with our circumstances, or do we go about giving the impression that we have been cheated and that we deserve much better?

It is this very matter of having an excellent spirit that carries so much promise for the church. If unbelievers are surprised by us, they will be willing to listen to us. If they can see that we are not like everyone else, they will have to wonder why and demand an explanation. If they see us being kind and forgiving even when we have reasons to be angry and resentful, they will have to give credence to our testimony.

We can win the argument with unbelievers without winning the unbelievers. We can explain the evidences for Christ and answer their objections regarding the truth of the Bible only to see them reject it all because our lives put before them an insurmountable obstacle.

Some Christians will never be able to win their employers to faith because they are such poor employees—always late, always sullen and complaining, always using company time for personal business or for surfing the Internet. Other Christians will never be able to win their children to faith because they have such a poor attitude towards the Lord, his church and the appointed leaders of the church!

On and on we could go! If we want to make a difference, let's show a difference, remembering the call of the apostle Paul to 'adorn the doctrine of God' in all things (Titus 2:10).

THE PERIL OF EXCELLENCE

Having a spirit that goes beyond the typical human spirit carries great promise in the matter of convincing unbelievers. But it also carries peril, as Daniel 6 shows. The excellent spirit will never fail to make people think about God, and there are many who cannot be reminded of God without becoming angry.

Daniel's excellent spirit had this effect on the other governors and the satraps. His excellent spirit set him out and put him in line for promotion, and they hated him for it. But more than that, they hated him because, in the words of Ronald S. Wallace, 'Daniel never failed to let it be known to all around him that what was "most excellent" about him derived not from Babylon itself, but from Jerusalem, to whose culture and religion he turned constantly for inspiration.'[1]

In other words, the whole orientation of Daniel's life was towards Jerusalem, even though he lived in Babylon. His life stands as a reminder to Christians today that our orientation is always to be towards heaven even though we live upon this earth.

Hating Daniel, his excellent spirit and everything he stood for, the other governors and the satraps immediately set out to find a way to discredit him in the eyes of Darius.

A scheme soon suggested itself to them. They would convince Darius to forbid the offering of any prayer or any petition to any god or man except himself for a period of thirty days. Failure to comply would be punished by the offender being cast into a den of lions.

This scheme was undoubtedly presented to Darius as a sincere attempt to honour his greatness, but it had nothing to do with Darius. These officials knew Daniel would not comply and they could, therefore, rid themselves of him.

It's interesting that they manipulated the political system to murder Daniel. Have there been attempts in recent years to manipulate our political systems in such a way as to make life difficult for Christians?

The manoeuvrings of Daniel 6 seem on the surface to be nothing more than a political struggle, but one cannot help but see in it a deep and abiding antagonism towards Daniel because of his excellent spirit. Centuries later, Jesus of Nazareth stepped onto the stage of human history with an even more excellent spirit than Daniel. And that excellent spirit caused him to be so hated that his enemies crucified him.

But no one with an excellent spirit ever loses. Daniel didn't, and the Lord Jesus didn't either. The very crucifixion his enemies used to kill him became the means by which God saves sinners and gives them eternal life.

Let us learn from Daniel and Jesus to strive for that excellent spirit, knowing, no matter what it costs, that it will be well worth possessing and will finally be rewarded fully in eternity itself.

FOR FURTHER STUDY

1. The book of Esther describes another king issuing a decree to cause the deaths of God's people. Who was he? Why did he issue the decree? How was it thwarted?

2. Read Psalm 2. What parallels do you see between this psalm and Daniel 6?

TO THINK ABOUT AND DISCUSS

1. Some attitudes that are typical of the human spirit were listed above. Can you think of others?

2. Name some other people in the Bible, from both the Old and New Testaments, who manifested an 'excellent spirit'. How did they demonstrate this spirit through the circumstances and opposition they faced? What lessons for your own life and circumstances can you learn from them?

Note

1 **Wallace,** p. 106.

11 A pattern to follow and a picture to admire

Daniel 6:10–28

Daniel lived the kind of life that should have won him lots of friends and no enemies. It was a life of pristine beauty. But Daniel had his enemies! There were lots of people in the Medo-Persian Empire who hated him. Some of it was due to jealousy. Men wanted the recognition that came to Daniel without living the kind of life that earned the recognition!

Even more of it, however, was this Jerusalem thing! Even though Daniel was far removed from Jerusalem, he brought Jerusalem and all it represented with him into Babylon.

Daniel believed in one God, and he believed that men and women can do nothing to make themselves acceptable to God. He believed that men and women must receive the grace of God or be eternally lost.

People still hate to be told that there is such a thing as finality in religion. And they hate to be told that there is only one way to be saved. Tell them that there are lots of truths and lots of ways to be saved, and they are happy. But insist on one God and one way to God, and they get really angry!

So the haters of Daniel decided to do away with him, and the means they chose for doing so was the political system. They would manipulate the system to murder Daniel.

How did these men manipulate the system? As we have seen, they convinced Darius to sign a decree that all prayers should be addressed to him for a period of thirty days. Anyone who failed to comply would be thrown into a den of lions (vv. 6–7).

It is interesting that they put a time limit on it. They didn't want Darius to make the decree permanent! They didn't want him to get the idea that he was some sort of god! They only wanted to use him to get rid of Daniel.

The thought appealed to Darius, and, without thinking of the effect it would have upon Daniel, he signed the decree. Now the fat was in the fire! A decree of the king could not be changed or altered. It had to be carried out (v. 8). So Daniel had to quit praying to God or be thrown to the lions. His enemies must have rubbed their hands in glee. They had Daniel right where they wanted him! They knew he would not quit praying to God, and they now had a decree that outlawed such praying, a decree that could not be changed!

A PATTERN TO BE FOLLOWED

When Daniel learned about the writing, he did exactly what his enemies expected. He prayed to God (v. 10). Here we have the key to his greatness. Daniel, this colossus of a man, was willing to be a child before God, humbly asking for his favour.

One part of his praying is emphasized in particular, namely his giving thanks to God. Here is a man who is headed into real trouble, and he still finds reasons to thank God! Is there anything for us to learn from this?

Some are troubled by the fact that Daniel seemed to make a

show of his praying. But this is not the case. The windows of that day were very high. The only way that Daniel's enemies could know about his spiritual disciplines was by getting someone to spy on him. This would have posed no problem for them since Daniel, as a high-ranking official, would have had lots of servants in his house.

The key question is whether we will let Daniel speak to us about the importance of setting and keeping spiritual disciplines. Will we let him speak especially about setting for ourselves the discipline of prayer?

There is no greater need this day than for Christians to be disciplined, and there is no point at which we need to be more disciplined than prayer. And there is no point at which we are more challenged by the devil than prayer. As the following lines indicate, the devil has no shortage of voices calling us from prayer:

Christian! dost thou hear them,
How they speak thee fair?
'Always fast and vigil?
Always watch and prayer?'

How should we respond to these voices? The same hymn gives the answer:

Christian! answer boldly,
'While I breathe I pray';
Peace shall follow battle,
Night shall end in day.[1]

Daniel prayed three times a day, not because it was commanded, but because he knew the value of spiritual discipline. It was not a matter of legalism—earning favour in the eyes of God; it was rather a matter of taking pleasure in God and making himself useful to God.

What effect would it have on others if we were to take pleasure in spiritual disciplines? What effect would it have if we were to set for ourselves the discipline of prayer? The question before many of us is not 'Will we pray when it is very costly to do so?' but rather 'Will we pray when it is easy to do so?'

When Daniel's praying was reported, Darius had no choice but to follow his own decree and throw Daniel into the lions' den (vv. 12–17). He was, however, greatly agitated that he had allowed himself to be tricked into setting a trap for the man he respected so much (v. 18). The king did console himself with the possibility that the God whom Daniel served would protect him from the lions (v. 16).

Early in the morning he rushed to the lions' den to see if his hope had been realized (v. 19). His heart must have leaped for joy when he heard Daniel say, 'My God sent His angel and shut the lions' mouths, so that they have not hurt me' (v. 22).

The God who made this world, and all the lions in it, has no trouble coming into his world to shut the mouths of his lions.

This passage does not entitle us to conclude that every child of God will always be spared from death. God doesn't always reward faithfulness in the same way. Sometimes faithfulness to God causes Christians to lose their lives, as was the case with Stephen (Acts 7:59), James (Acts 12:1–2) and Paul (2 Tim. 4:6). But God always rewards faithfulness in some way.

A PICTURE TO BE ADMIRED

We cannot leave this passage without thinking about the Lord Jesus Christ, who is so perfectly anticipated and pictured by Daniel.

Jesus stepped onto the stage of human history some 500 years after Daniel. He lived a far better life than Daniel. While Daniel was faithful to God in so many ways, he was still a flawed and imperfect man. But Jesus lived in perfect obedience to God.

His life of faithfulness caused Jesus to be hated just as Daniel was. And the haters of Jesus used their political power to condemn Jesus to death, just as Daniel's enemies used their political power.

We can go further. There is a significant connection between the way in which Daniel was condemned to death and the way in which Jesus was condemned to death. The condemnation of Daniel came about because Darius was caught in a dilemma created by his own law. That law required the death of Daniel, whom Darius earnestly desired to save but could not. The condemnation of Jesus also came about because God was caught, if we may picture it in this way, in a 'dilemma' created by his own law.

While the law of Darius was ill-advised, the law of God was just and holy. It was the law that sinners should be eternally separated from God because of their sins. Because God is merciful and kind, however, he desired to spare sinners just as Darius desired to spare Daniel.

So God's 'dilemma' was how to carry out the sentence he had pronounced upon sinners and, at the same time, allow those sinners to go free. Jesus is the answer to that dilemma. He went to the cross for the express purpose of receiving the sentence God pronounced on sinners. Because Jesus received it, there is no penalty left for all those who believe in him.

That brings us to a final parallel between Daniel and Jesus. Jesus was not spared death as Daniel was, but he was delivered from it. Just as Daniel was lifted from the lions' den, so Jesus was lifted from the grave on the third day.

Because Jesus arose from the grave, we know that he is everything that he claimed to be and that we must flee to him as our Lord and Saviour.

For further study ▶

FOR FURTHER STUDY

1. Read Psalm 64. What parallels do you see between this psalm and Daniel 6?
2. Read John 8:38–47. How did Jesus explain the hatred the religious leaders had for him?

TO THINK ABOUT AND DISCUSS

1. What steps can you take to become more disciplined in prayer? Are there other spiritual disciplines that you could improve—for example, Bible reading and reading Christian books?
2. Identify some ways in which governments today seek to manipulate the political system to bring distress to God's people. What lessons can we learn from the life of Daniel about how we should respond to these challenges?

Note

1 **Andrew of Crete,** 'Christian! Dost Thou See Them', 7th cent.; trans. John Mason Neale, 1862.

12 The delights of faith

Daniel 9:1–19

We pick up the thread of the narrative of Daniel in these verses. The non-narrative portions (7:1–8:27; 9:20–12:13) consist of various visions Daniel received. While these visions fall outside the scope of our study, they are very important in that they show us that God is in control. He knows in advance what is going to take place. Furthermore, he is bringing all the turbulent details of history to the end that he has appointed, and that end is achieved through the redeeming work of Christ.

It is now the year 537 BC. Daniel, who was taken captive by the Babylonians when he was young, is now an old man; yet his faith is new. Stuart Olyott writes of Daniel, 'Many years have passed since he last saw Jerusalem, but the old man's faith is as fresh as ever. Trials have not broken it. Promotion has not eroded it or seduced him to love other things more than his God.'[1]

How do we know that Daniel's faith had not grown old and tired? Our passage gives us the answer. Even at his advanced age, Daniel was still doing those things that faith delights itself in.

Do you want to know the condition of your faith? Do you want to know whether your faith is still new and fresh or stagnant and stale? Here is the test: are you still doing those things in which faith delights?

What are the delights of faith? Our passage leaves no doubt about the answer. Faith delights in reading and studying the Word of God and in approaching the throne of God in prayer.

FAITH DELIGHTING IN THE BIBLE

As the chapter opens, we find Daniel studying the Word of God as it was delivered through Jeremiah the prophet. He is reading the scroll of Jeremiah (vv. 1–2).

We should never minimize the significance of Daniel reading the Word of God. Stuart Olyott explains, 'Daniel was a great prophet and had had many remarkable visions and revelations, but he never outgrew the need to read his Bible.'[2]

Christian, it doesn't matter how long you live and how far advanced you become in spiritual things. You will never outgrow your Bible! The Bible is not only milk for the new Christian, it is also meat for the most advanced Christian. It is not only the kindergarten for the saints, it is also the graduate school!

David was a very saintly and godly man, but he never outgrew his Bible either. He said to the Lord, 'Your word is a lamp to my feet and a light to my path' (Ps. 119:105). He also said, 'I rejoice at Your word as one who finds great treasure' (Ps. 119:162).

Have you outgrown your Bible? If you have, you can be assured that your faith will shrivel up, and when you need it, it will not be there to sustain you. Faith has to have food, and the food for faith is the Word of God (Rom. 10:17).

As Daniel studied the prophecy of Jeremiah, he found

something that took his breath away. Jeremiah declared that the Jews' captivity in Babylon would last for seventy years (Jer. 25:8–11; 29:10–14). As Daniel read, he quickly realized that almost all those years had already passed! The time Jeremiah had predicted was almost over!

Had Daniel never read this before? Or had he read it without really seeing it? We cannot say, but on this occasion, it fairly leaped off the page at Daniel.

One reason to read the Bible is that we never know when the same thing will happen to us. We never know when something that has been there all along will leap up to grab us and thrill us!

FAITH DELIGHTING IN PRAYER

The Bible constantly sets before us the vital importance of prayer. It does so in more than one way. Sometimes it simply commands us to pray. At other times it gives us examples of prayer from the greatest saints of God. If these men needed to pray, how much more do we!

Verses 3–10 of our chapter give us the prayer of Daniel, one of the saintliest men of all time. We do well to read it carefully and to seek to emulate it.

We also do well to remember that Daniel began praying because of what he read in the Word of God. The attitude of many would be along these lines: if God promised it, there is no reason to pray. Daniel's attitude was: if God has promised it, there is even more reason to pray. Stuart Olyott says, 'Whatever other lessons we learn from this chapter, we must be sure to grasp this one. The cause of God's acting in history is not simply His promise, but also the prayer of His people.'[3]

Prayer in its highest form is seeking that which God has promised to bestow. This enables us to pray with confidence and assurance.

THE WAY IN WHICH DANIEL PRAYED

Daniel did not go about his praying in a casual, nonchalant way; he poured himself into it. He 'set' his face 'toward the Lord God' (v. 3). And he did so with fasting, sackcloth and ashes.

THE PRAYER DANIEL OFFERED

It was first a prayer of adoration and praise (vv. 4, 9). Daniel did not merely rush into the presence of God and start making his requests known; he began by offering worship and praise. God is Lord. He is 'great and awesome' (v. 4). He is faithful and merciful (v. 4). He is forgiving (v. 9).

Let's learn from Daniel that the proper way to begin prayer is with the worship of Almighty God. Yes, we have our needs and our pressing concerns, and we are very anxious to pour them all out in a torrent to the Lord. But no matter how urgent and pressing the need, it is still proper to begin with adoration and praise. The believers in the early church knew this. The authorities were breathing down their necks and the need was urgent and great, but they still began their praying with worship (Acts 4:23–31).

If we will insist on beginning our prayers in this manner, we shall find that we are doing ourselves more good than we realize. If we begin by occupying ourselves with God and his greatness, we shall soon find our problems shrinking in size.

Our problems, no matter how great, are not as great as our God!

Having offered praise to God, Daniel turned to the sinful condition of himself and his people.

What is sin? It is failing to live according to what God has commanded in his Word. It is failing to do what he has told us to do ('walk in His laws', v. 10), and it is doing what he has told us not to do ('departed so as not to obey Your voice', v. 11).

True repentance not only confesses sin but also honours God in judging sin (v. 11). It takes God's side against sin and pronounces his judgement to be right.

Having worshipped God and confessed the sins of his people, Daniel turned his attention to supplication (vv. 16–19). In this part of his prayer, Daniel pleaded with God to:
- turn away from anger (v. 16);
- hear his prayer (vv. 17–19);
- cause his face to shine again on his sanctuary (v. 17);
- see the desolations of Jerusalem (v. 18);
- not delay (v. 19);
- act for the sake of his own name (v. 19).

While there is an intensity and depth of feeling that runs throughout Daniel's prayer, it is especially apparent in this portion. It is also important to notice that Daniel recognized that he and his people had no merit to plead but could only plead for the mercy of God.

Does this not bring us face to face with one of the most glaring deficiencies in our praying and one of the reasons why our praying seems to accomplish so very little? How much intensity do we have in our praying? How much of this element of pleading do we have?

So Daniel delighted himself in the Word of God and in prayer. There is not much glamour in reading the Word of God and in praying, and many in the church have moved on to other things. But God has not moved on! He still delights in them, and we must delight in them as well. The measure of our faith is not to be found in ecstasies and emotional experiences, but rather in the degree to which we delight in Bible study and prayer.

The church of today sorely needs true spiritual renewal. But let us not be in doubt about what a genuine revival will do. It will sweep away a thousand things that churches are now doing and will place on centre stage the Bible and prayer.

The passage we have been considering does not end the book of Daniel. The remaining chapters relate an additional vision and prophecies. But we take our leave of Daniel at a good point—a good man doing the good work of studying God's Word and approaching God's throne in prayer. May God help all of us who share Daniel's faith to follow his example until that glorious day when we arise to our inheritance (12:13) and meet Daniel face to face.

FOR FURTHER STUDY

1. Why should we value God's Word? See Psalm 119:1–2, 9, 11, 45, 105, 130. What will we do with God's Word if we truly value it? See Psalm 119:2–16.

2. Read Ephesians 3:20. What does this verse teach us about prayer? How does this encourage you?

TO THINK ABOUT AND DISCUSS

1. Conduct a spiritual inventory to determine whether your faith has grown old and tired. Think not only about the amount of time you spend in Bible study and prayer, but also about the degree to which you relish such times. Think also about your attitude towards public worship. If you find that you are cold towards these things, what do you need to do?

2. What have you learned about prayer from this chapter? How will you change your prayer habits as a result?

Notes

1 **Olyott,** pp. 115–116.
2 Ibid. p. 116.
3 Ibid. p. 118.

About Day One:

Day One's threefold commitment:

- TO BE FAITHFUL TO THE BIBLE, GOD'S INERRANT, INFALLIBLE WORD;

- TO BE RELEVANT TO OUR MODERN GENERATION;

- TO BE EXCELLENT IN OUR PUBLICATION STANDARDS.

I continue to be thankful for the publications of Day One. They are biblical; they have sound theology; and they are relative to the issues at hand. The material is condensed and manageable while, at the same time, being complete—a challenging balance to find. We are happy in our ministry to make use of these excellent publications.

JOHN MACARTHUR, PASTOR-TEACHER, GRACE COMMUNITY CHURCH, CALIFORNIA

It is a great encouragement to see Day One making such excellent progress. Their publications are always biblical, accessible and attractively produced, with no compromise on quality. Long may their progress continue and increase!

JOHN BLANCHARD, AUTHOR, EVANGELIST AND APOLOGIST

Visit our website for more information and to request a free catalogue of our books.
www.dayone.co.uk
www.dayonebookstore.com

Face2face series

Title	Author	ISBN
Face2face David Volume 1	Michael Bentley	978–1–84625–040–8
Face2face David Volume 2	Michael Bentley	978–1–84625–015–6
Face2face Elijah	Simon J Robinson	978–1–84625–011–8
Face2face Elisha	Jim Winter	978–1–84625–113–9
Face2face Rahab	Chris Hughes	978–1–84625–135–1
Face2face Samuel	Roger Ellsworth	978–1–84625–039–2
Face2face Sennacherib	Clive Anderson	978–1–84625–076–7
Face2face Simon Peter	Roger Ellsworth	978–1–84625–092–7
Face2face Tamar, Bathsheba and Tamar	Julia Jones	978–1–84625–141–2

Face2face with Samuel—Encountering the king-maker

ROGER ELLSWORTH

128PP, PAPERBACK

ISBN 978–1–84625–039–2

Welcome to the world of dirt roads and oxcarts, cattle and sheep, sandals and robes! Welcome to the world of Samuel—one of the most important men in the history of the nation of Israel. Samuel was a great prophet occupying a unique position in the history of his nation. For a long time, Israel had been ruled by 'judges', but Samuel ushered them into a new era in which they were governed by kings. However, we are not taking this 'face2face' look at Samuel because we are interested in his historical uniqueness but rather because he can help us to know the God who made us and who has a wonderful purpose for all who live for him.

Roger Ellsworth has served as pastor of Immanuel Baptist Church, Benton, Illinois, for eighteen years. He is the author of twenty-seven books, including *Opening up Philippians* and *Opening up Psalms*.

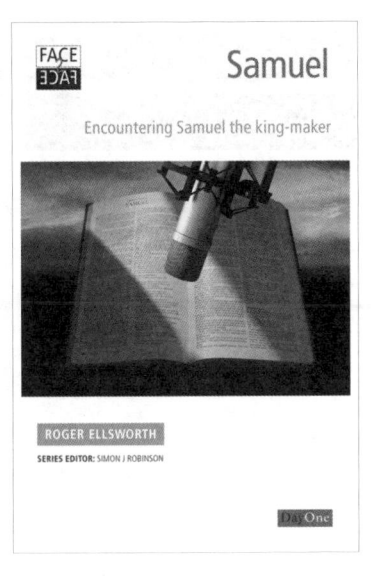

'Roger Ellsworth's book is an extremely relevant and helpful study in the life of Samuel, a much-neglected Old Testament character. It is an extremely practical, pastoral and, most important of all, Christ-exalting-character study at its best and an invaluable addition to a promising series.'

DEREK PRIME

FACE2FACE: DANIEL

Face to face with David volume 1— Encountering the man after God's heart

MICHAEL BENTLEY

96PP, PAPERBACK

ISBN 978-1-84625-040-8

Raised in obscurity, young David would not have featured on a list of candidates for the future king of Israel-but God had different ideas! Read, here, about how God's magnificent plan unfolded in the life of this remarkable man and in the lives of those around him.

Michael Bentley worked as a bookshop manager and served in the British army before his call to the ministry. He has a diverse background, which includes broadcasting, teaching Religious Education, and holding pastorates in Surrey, South East London, and Berkshire, while being closely involved with his local community. Now retired, he lives in Bracknell with his wife, Jenny, and has five children and six grandchildren. He is the author of ten books.

Michael Bentley has an enviable knowledge of the Bible and an admirably simple way of relating its events, and then interweaving the stories with their relevance to our life. Thus, we see how the actions related in the bible can still be appropriate today in the way we live our lives.

FRAN GODFREY, BBC RADIO 2 NEWSREADER/ANNOUNCER

FACE**2**FACE: DANIEL

Face to face David volume 2—Encountering the king who reigned in power

MICHAEL BENTLEY

144PP, PAPERBACK

ISBN 978–1–84625–015–6

Raised in obscurity, shooting to prominence in the nation of Israel, David became a powerful figure and everyone loved him—well, not quite everyone. Read about his battles, his triumphs, and also his troubles in this engaging, easy-to-use guide.

Michael Bentley worked as a bookshop manager and served in the British army before his call to the ministry. He has a diverse background, which includes broadcasting, teaching Religious Education, and holding pastorates in Surrey, South East London, and Berkshire, while being closely involved with his local community. Now retired, he lives in Bracknell with his wife, Jenny, and has five children and six grandchildren. He is the author of ten books.

'Michael Bentley treats the life of David in a simple, straightforward fashion, never losing sight throughout of the practical significance he has for us, and constantly holding before us David's greater Son, the Lord Jesus. A very good and satisfying book!'
ROGER ELLSWORTH, PASTOR OF IMMANUEL BAPTIST CHURCH, BENTON, ILLINOIS, USA, AND BIBLE COMMENTATOR

'... a book which is full of wisdom ...'
CHRIS PORTER, MINISTER, EASTHAMPSTEAD BAPTIST CHURCH, ENGLAND

FACE2FACE: DANIEL

Face to face Sennacherib—Encountering Assyria's great and terrifying ruler

CLIVE ANDERSON

96PP, PAPERBACK

ISBN 978–1–84625–076–7

Sennacherib was once a name to send a chill down spines, yet today, relatively few have heard of him, and even fewer know much about him. Lord Byron immortalized one part of his life in a poem, but there was much more to this man than King and fearsome warrior. Coming face to face with him in this book not only reveals a complex and multi-talented man, but also the formidable enemy that the land of Judah, its king Hezekiah and prophet Isaiah were confronted with at a time of national crisis.

Today, many Christians across the world find themselves faced with situations that appear to be beyond their control. How should they react in such circumstances and what help can they expect to receive? This book, while dealing with real history, also focuses on life in the twenty-first century and gives pointers towards being faithful witnesses of Jesus Christ.

Clive Anderson is the pastor of the Butts Church in Alton, Hampshire, and a member of The British Museum Society, The British School of Archaeology in Iraq, and The Egyptian Exploration Society, and leads tours to the Middle East and Egypt and around the British Museum. He is the author of *Opening up Nahum*, *Opening up 2 Peter*, *Travel with Spurgeon*, *Gunpowder, Treason and Plot*, and has co-authored with Brian Edwards

Through the British Museum with the Bible, all published by Day One. Clive had spoken in the USA, Europe, and in the Far East, and is also a frequent broadcaster on local radio. He and his wife, Amanda, have one son.

'Clive Anderson brings ancient history to life. Out of the stony slabs of antiquity, Sennacherib emerges, flesh and blood. Using biblical sources and drawing on his extensive knowledge of archaeology and ancient history, Clive Anderson gives the reader a fascinating insight into the life and times of this notorious Assyrian king—enriching and sharpening our understanding of the biblical text. This book is a must for preachers and teachers and an invaluable aid to Bible study. It is easily accessible scholarship—providing accurate background knowledge, sound biblical exposition and searching application.'
REV. DR JIM WINTER, PASTOR, HORSELL EVANGELICAL CHURCH, AND AUTHOR OF SEVERAL BOOKS

'Clive Anderson brings two great passions to bear in the writing of this book. The first is that by filling in the blanks of our map of Old Testament history the key points which God highlights would be better seen and understood by God's people. The second is that from a clearer understanding of God's dealings with his people would flow a clearer desire to walk in God's ways. Both passions are plain to see throughout this book and applied with insight and wisdom by a very knowledgeable and passionate writer.'
CHRIS HUGHES, PASTOR OF BISHOPSTOKE EVANGELICAL CHURCH, HAMPSHIRE, ENGLAND

'A gem of a book'
REV. DR IAIN D CAMPBELL

FACE2FACE: DANIEL

Face to face with Elijah—Encountering Elijah the fiery prophet

SIMON J ROBINSON

80PP, PAPERBACK

ISBN 978-1-84625-011-8

Elijah, the fiery prophet, lived in a time of intense spiritual darkness. People were openly disobeying God's commands, and true worship seemed to have been all but snuffed out. And yet God was still at work! Bringing the power of his word and Spirit into this situation, he used Elijah to break the darkness and to draw people back to himself. This fascinating encounter with Elijah draws out his significance in God's plan and provides us with practical help to live for Christ in the spiritual darkness of the twenty-first century. Each chapter includes questions and points for reflection, making this an ideal book to be used in small groups or for personal study and devotion.

Simon Robinson is the senior minister of Walton Evangelical Church, Chesterfield, England. He has also written several other books, all published by Day One, including *Jesus, the life-changer, Improving your quiet time, Opening up 1 Timothy,* and *God, the Bible and terrorism*. He also preaches and teaches in Asia and the United States. He and his wife, Hazel, have two sons and one grandson.

FACE**2**FACE: DANIEL